FOOTBALL

FOOTBALL: THE FUNDAMENTALS

BRYANT LLOYD

The Rourke Book Co., Inc.
Vero Beach, Florida 32964

EDITORIAL SERVICES:
Penworthy Learning Systems

Library of Congress Cataloging-in-Publication Data

Lloyd, Bryant. 1942
   Football: the fundamentals / by Bryant Lloyd.
       p. cm. — (Football)
   Includes index
   Summary: Describes the fundamental aspects of football, including the coaching, the teams, and such moves as blocking, passing, tackling, and kicking.
       ISBN 1-55916-215-5 (alk. paper)
       1. Football—Juvenile literature. [1. Football.] I. Title II. Series
GV950.7.L55 1997
796.332—dc21   97–777
                                                                CIP
                                                                AC

Printed in the USA

TABLE OF CONTENTS

THE GAME OF FOOTBALL

Tackle football is a rough and exciting game played between two teams. The game is timed by an official clock.

Football is played on a flat field, usually outdoors. The game is played throughout the United States and in parts of Canada.

Most football games in the United States are played between two teams of eleven boys or young men. Canadian football teams have 12 players on each side.

Football is usually played in autumn. The National Football League (NFL) schedule of professional games continue into winter.

The American Football League won the 1970 Super Bowl when the New York Jets beat the Baltimore Colts, 16-7. Jets' quarterback Joe Namath became a hero. He said before the game that his team would upset the National Football League's Colts.

Football is an exciting contact game played between two teams of 11 players each (Canadian football has 12 on a side).

GETTING READY FOR FOOTBALL

Football is demanding. It requires teamwork, speed, strength, and skill. Football players spend many hours getting ready for games.

Players exercise to make their bodies strong. Football exercises include stretching, weight lifting, running, and other activities.

Drills help football players learn skills and teamwork.

*Exercises help prepare players for the hard physical
contact of football.*

Football players also prepare by practicing
football plays. By **drilling** (DRIL ing), or
repeating plays over and over, football teams
sharpen their skills and ability to play together.

COACHING

One or more coaches direct each football team. The head coach is in charge of the team.

Coaches decide which position a player will play. They teach the player how best to play that position. The coach decides when a player on the field should be replaced by another player.

Football teams use many different plays to move the ball forward. A coach usually decides which play the team will use.

A coach helps the team form a plan for the game and make it work.

THE TEAMS

The football team with the ball is the **offensive** (AW fen siv) team. Its job is to move the football forward, closer to or across the **defensive** (DEE fen siv) team's goal line. The defensive team tries to stop the offensive team.

When a kicking play is called for, the teams on the field are often called special teams.

A football player usually plays either on his team's offense, defense, or special team. A few players play on two or three units.

The first Super Bowl game was played in 1967, between the Green Bay Packers and Kansas City Chiefs. The Packers won 35-10 and defeated the Oakland Raiders in the 1968 Super Bowl game.

Offensive team (yellow jerseys) tries to move ball forward to cross the defensive team's goal line.

BLOCKING

Most players on the offensive team must **block** (BLAHK). A player blocks by using his body to keep a defensive player away from the ball carrier. Certain rules apply to how a player can block.

Three-point stance—one hand and two feet braced on the ground—helps blockers get a good push forward.

Offensive player (86) holds off defensive player with a block. Number 71 rushes to set up another block for team's running back (21), who is about to take ball from quarterback.

Blocking helps clear a path through which a ball carrier can run. A block may be no more than a brush against someone. It may also be a very forceful bump or push with the shoulders. Good blocking often begins from a crouch called a three-point **stance** (STANS) (see picture).

RUNNING WITH THE BALL

The offensive team usually gains yards on the field by running the football forward or passing it from one player to another.

When running, a ball carrier takes the football and tries to rush through the defensive players. As the runner moves forward, he may shift the football from one hand to the other. He wants to keep the ball away from the closest tackler.

The runner can use his free hand and arm as a stiff-arm—to push away a tackler.

Touch football, like flag football, requires no tackling or bulky equipment. Touch football requires only that a defensive player make contact with the ball carrier to stop the play.

Runner shifts ball to right hand as tackler rushes up.

PASSING THE BALL

When a team passes, it advances the football by throwing it forward. One player, usually the **quarterback** (KWAWR ter bak), passes the ball to another offensive player. The ball may be thrown any distance.

The player catching the football is the **receiver** (ree SEE ver). The receiver can run until he is tackled.

If the pass is not caught, the play ends. Defensive players are free to catch the quarterback's pass, too, and run toward the offense's goal line.

Quarterback (black jersey, center) throws pass downfield to a receiver.

TACKLING

The defensive team stops the offense by tackling its ball carrier or chasing him out of bounds. Defenders may have to push or pull blockers out of their way to reach the ball carrier.

With left arm locked around a leg, tackler (white jersey, on ground) brings down the ball carrier.

Hard-driving tackle with shoulder and arms knocks the ball carrier backward.

Tacklers try to wrap their arms around the ball carrier's legs and knock him over. Knocking the ball carrier to the ground ends the play. The teams then return to their sides of the ball before play begins again.

KICKING

The football may be kicked at many different times in a game. A place kicker kicks the ball from the ground. A punter kicks the ball in mid-air after dropping it from his hands.

Kicking is one way to score points. It is also the common way for the offense to turn the ball over to the defense.

Most kickers kick, or boot, the ball from the inside of their foot, soccer-style. A punter kicks from the top of his foot.

College and professional football games are played in four 15-minute quarters. The games last much longer than one hour, though, because the clock stops after certain kinds of plays.

Place kicker swings foot into the football resting on a kicking tee.

GLOSSARY

block (BLAHK) — physical contact made by an offensive player to stop the progress of a defensive player; the act of making contact to stop or slow a defensive player

defensive (DEE fen siv) — on the defense; to be in the position of defender

drilling (DRIL ing) — repeating something over and over to increase skill or strength

offensive (AW fen siv) — on the offense; referring to the team with the ball; being on the attack

quarterback (KWAWR ter bak) — the offensive team's player who calls plays and directs the football

receiver (ree SEE ver) — any player who catches a forward pass; one who sets up in a football formation as if he might catch a pass

stance (STANS) — a position one takes, especially the position of football players blocking on the line of scrimmage

Sportsmanship should be a part of every football game. Game over, players exchange high fives in a show of respect for each other.

INDEX